*I Am a City Still
But Soon I Shan't Be*

Other books by Roger Farr

Surplus (2006)
Means (2010)
IKMQ (2012)

I Am a City Still
But Soon I Shan't Be

ROGER FARR

Vancouver :: New Star Books :: 2019

New Star Books Ltd.
107 – 3477 Commercial Street, Vancouver, BC V5N 4E8 CANADA
1574 Gulf Road, No. 1517, Point Roberts, WA 98281 USA
www.NewStarBooks.com ◆ info@NewStarBooks.com

The publisher acknowledges the financial support of the Canada Council for the Arts and the British Columbia Arts Council.

Cataloguing information for this book is available from Library and Archives Canada, www.collectionscanada.gc.ca.

Cover design and book by Clint Hutzulak / Rayola Creative
Printed and bound in Canada by Imprimerie Gauvin, Gatineau, QC

Published September 2019

When the Stranger says: "What is the meaning of this city?
Do you huddle close together because you love each other?"
What will you answer? "We all dwell together
To make money from each other"? or "This is a community"?
And the Stranger will depart and return to the desert.

– T. S. Eliot, *Choruses from The Rock*

1
Liquidity

Did you feel that surge spread across
    the room the sector the city Monday morning
current rising violently to a foaming shot
    over the precincts up against the wall
every body open and quivering despite
    the security presence the infrastructure
losing contour losing investors losing coherency
    seeping at last into the gaping ear of the social body?

I did. Hailed by the Call as I stepped across
    Venables at Clark following a transverse line
like all the other commodities circulating aimlessly
    I drifted along corrugated steel walls
sun burning every body every building every form
    cash exploding from crowns of distant towers
occupied by the *rentiers* in this haemopolis of
    arteries and conduits branching out centrifugally.

Day broke over the grid of inputs outputs
    pipelines fibre-optic cables electrodes.
The citizens looked scorched and picked over
    as they transited through the subway tunnels
into the pits. The air was thin and material.
    The fluorescent glare illuminating the cheque-
cashing outlet brought the pallid face of austerity
    into view — the deeply etched scowl

Eyes darting fingers twitching never enough
　　　never enough never enough. Immigration goons
patrolled the entrances at the periphery while
　　　snipers positioned themselves tactically
behind the billboards. Aerial surveillance
　　　rigid architectural controls and yet *my* passage
between sectors was as fluid as the debt relation
　　　that governed it. This is a black and white film

And we are the extras. The script is based on
        a poem by Nietzsche called *Schuld*. I paused
on the viaduct to petition the souls of those
        who died when their neighborhood was flooded
by a violent stream of capital during a previous
        cycle of struggle. Fear death by finance.
Such lessons of history bore down upon me
        as I surveyed the landscape for signs

Of the raging stream the undercurrent the urgency
        tunneling beneath this unceded land. Derelict
buildings tilted dramatically into an eroding
        riverbed while municipal road crews labored
to repair the damaged infrastructure. My eye
        scanned horizontally across the metropolis
before gazing vertically into its past.
        Shipping containers moved East and West

Without obstruction. Today the surfaces
of assent appear smooth and dry. Tomorrow
may be a sequel. Under the cranes the citizen
dreams itself a protagonist signing land title
papers in a parking lot on the Eastside
stocks ripening in the temperate rain.
At the "moment of contact" this city swallowed
its own imago the dead conjured the living

And the living conjured a utopia of glass. I crossed
    the street and entered a receding alley. The world
drifted away. It seemed I was the only pedestrian
    in a corridor delineated by garbage and recycling
bins. On every surface a riot of ciphers and slogans
    passwords insults spells provided ludic commentary
on the internal contradictions of the structure
    that enclosed me. The names of local snitches

Were on display. Educated stencil artists had left
    their meta-commentary too but what delayed my eye
were the almost invisible instructions on how to
    stay alive how to live during a period of civil war.
Ahead of me the mass of commuters and customers
    shuffled back and forth across the aperture
at the end of the lane. Behind me the course extended
    down a hill and evaporated. I found myself caught

Between two fates: move forward and engage
    the crowd or turn and withdraw into quiet
contemplation. This inertia was overcome
    by velocity. I joined the others by force of current
and at that moment recalled a passage by Gleick —
    Any liquid or gas is a collection of individual bits.
If each piece moved independently then the fluid
    would have infinitely many possibilities

But each particle does not move independently —
    its motion depends very much on the motion
of its neighbours. Then another by Eberhardt
    on following two paths *one full of adventure*
that belongs in the desert another of calm
    and restful thought far away from all
that might interfere with it. I entered a park
    and saw a young woman with a Marseilles deck

Spread across a red cloth. I kneeled before her
and chose three cards. "You are at a crossroads
alone. You are a Hermit walking with your back
turned to the future. You cannot see your way.
Theory has failed you and so has the aesthetic
dulled down by data and entertainment. Why
do you look to the past? History is a nightmare
that can not help you now. You must become

What you hate and destroy what you love —
    an Emperor. Make physical changes.
Refuse work and take command of your life.
    Your project will require great Strength.
In your meager attempts to oppose authority
    you have lost your own *potência*. Embrace
your fighting spirit. *Affirm the value*
    of violence as the root of all power.

2
New Sensorium

Each desiring stream returns to its source. Entering

New York I began with practiced observations

about labour and finance and art but my taxonomy

was dull. The city in its Second Antebellum phase

had passed from *living laboratory* to elegant incubator

housing a colony of bacterial cultures that fed on

debt. Never before had I seen such a collection

of bare life. I had to recalibrate my instruments

To find a path through the mass of sour data
    I had cached. Hours spent in Street View had neutralized
the element of adventure only the aroma of anaerobic
    sewage waffles urine perfume mixed in nitrogen
fog and the fine light rain remained aesthetic. Oppen
    had said nothing about this — simply that the air was *stale*.
The *plume of smoke* in which the people burned was visible
    to him at a distance. Now it lingered in every station

Every outlet every gallery every cell. At the corner
     of Orchard and Delancey it lingered as a gang
of freshmen listening to deadmau5 strutted by.
     It lingered behind two old women pushing baby
carriages over hollow sidewalks while well-dressed
     figures of uncertain genders and class positions made
duck faces and laughed at the crowd outside Max Fish. A man
     holding a cocktail grinned through his grills

Exhaled it through his nose. The data accumulated
     as our stride widened. A sign in the window utters
"Breakfast Served Now" but the place is always closed.
     The statue of Eros in Albert's Garden cannot be seen
in photographs cannot become part of this ekphrasis.
     Trains enter stations. Light-bulbs are loosened. This
is how my desire works — the objects lead effortlessly to
     abstractions. Each singularity enclosed in an image

Shaped without stopping the passage of light is a monument
      to the bureaucracy of the senses. No ceremonial opening
of *the gates of perception* no *vast expanse* no panoramic
      money shot. I can portray only what is very close:
concealed doors in unfamiliar alleyways with ladders
      descending to meaningless bunkers people climbing up
and down the silicon membrane encasing a series of
      accidental encounters the inconstant odors the texture

Of the currency washing everything in a reality effect.

There was no entrance so there are no exits. Every morning
we turned right on Rivington and stood at the corner
contemplating rent my head cloudy from last night's
drink. At the local burlesque show it had become apparent
there was no such thing as a local. We were all spectators
to a post-pornographical return of the flesh. Rosie in red
asked if she could stand with us on our table. She lived

Around the corner but had never been there before
        handed me a drink through the crowd at the bar
and winked. The armor of identity sometimes constitutes
        a physical barrier between bodies in New York.
The new avant-gardes do not seek to close separations
        between art and life but to increase the divide between
the forms-of-life themselves. They do not make children.
        Their barricades are historical except they are composed

Of hybrids and polymers fastened with latex and lube
     not love. They are used to prevent the escape of the
police not to defend territory. This isn't another manifesto
     it's reported speech. The bacterial spores inside this fridge
communicate through mitosis and infect the sensory organs
     with their newish dithyrambic hostility. Whitman's
well-formed mechanics of Manhattan have given way
     to approximate lines measured by the square foot.

3
Flesh Passages

Our thinking is debris borne by a torrent
    but we can not say if the city was built
to channel a flow of blood or water or semen
    or cash or whether this metaphor this metabolism
has already run its course. Still I saw the warm
    bodies emerging from their incubators and drifting
through the ducts with ripening urgency
    and *ressentiment.* Some of us I noticed were

Slender tattooed brunettes in camouflage and tight
    black denim with tawny beards fringing our lips.
Into our orifices we inserted instruments words
    prosthetics anatomies in defiance in celebration
of every taboo every shame every code every
    father. Elevators departing from the carpeted foyers
of the high-rises lead to apartments decorated
    in powder. From this height I see everything

Except the end of the line: the districts located
    beyond the East-West paradigm the migrant desires
that arrive and depart with such certainty the zones
    of opacity that vanish under even the softest of
external controls. This is a libertine's war room
    partners swapping each other out for strangers
slaves whipped with ersatz phalluses husbands
    retreating to the corners pressing their vanilla

Asses hard against the cage as blindfolded subs
    perch on the furniture. By-law enforcement officers
dole out punishments for Failure to Use Safe Words.
    The blue light cast by a thousand surveillance cameras
illuminates some of the darker quadrants of the
    apartment and yet it seems this whole performance
is being staged entirely for the pleasure of the actors
    not the planners whose auto-eroticism is derived

From the contemplation of a single painting — a lewd
    image of a walled city undergoing reconstructive
surgery in a day clinic in Yaletown. I scan the room
    for an exit advance through the double French doors
off the swarming master bedroom find myself on
    a patio a subway platform among a familiar milieu
of fellow travellers following a line of flight away
    from the circuits of exchange. We undress each other

And begin to play while the train plunges beneath
    the pavement to follow — as all subterranean channels
do — a path of least resistance to the sea. Bodies lost
    their armour. I surveyed the full arc of a spine
shuddered in an alcove of soft pink tissue felt the blood-
    hardened organs swelling and driving as every tongue
every ear every limb every socket was expropriated
    and made common for a brief moment in time.

We disembarked amidst a zone of industrial ruins
    that lay before the beach. Everywhere the remainders
of the anthropocene formed an immense assemblage
    reminding us of something we had witnessed
in a film. As we probed this dystopia we caught glimpses
    on tiny screens flashing inside the decomposing chassis
strewn redundantly among lush stands of nettles black-
    berries and alder of the world we left behind:

Mid-winter crisis — suburbs' gyre widening
    isolated nuclear families frozen in their bunkers-
for-two all affections rationed power shut off
    booze hoarded nourishment kept to themselves as
the malls crumbled highways iced over shelters crowded
    squalid and curfewed. This was not a trailer for a projected
sequence of events but live footage of *a single catastrophe which
    keeps piling wreckage upon wreckage* before our eyes.

4
Interregnums

Hit the pause button on Köpenicker. Captured
    a woman carrying a turntable as she cut
into the Sage Club. Somehow the tactically sited
    billboard on the wall showed the exact same
figure pumping his car with gas from behind.
    Inside the club DJ Albertine nodded at a screen
while bodies pumped their sweaty torsos hard
    against the bass. Already alarms were rousing

The herd but a few of us still wandered the city
      trying to prolong the negation. The street lamps
buzzed and burned amid another blue chemical dawn.
      As in some necropolis it appeared we were a gang
of lucid mourners among four million dead. Shards of
      green glass strewn over the streets set the measure
for our dirge to the catastrophe of the singular.
      This was not a vision quest but a breathing

Space. We told ourselves we had to stop the sun
    or be captured by a job but to the cops we repeated
our refusals in the argot we had forged years ago
    in Brokdorf. The order that stretched around every
corner every artery every limb instructed us to feel
    not to think. Pausing later at Friedrichstrasse and
Dorotheenstrasse for the yellow tram to pass I
    felt nothing but thought this was significant —

I wanted more clanging among the variant bodies
	all washed in muted pastels pressing against me
each opening a potential line of flight — but nothing.
	Everything felt the same everywhere. I asked
in the *Journal* if hypoesthesia was a symptom of mass
	consent or yet another motif from the *Traumnovelle*
creeping into everyday life. If only the DJ in the club
	or some other figure cut from a future passage

Could open narrative time by intimating the arrival of
   a secret orgy then maybe the breaks between the wards
not their shared atmosphere would allow us to hear
   the new dialect warbling through the cables.
The yellow tram passed. I found myself driven forward
   believing my passage was free but once again I
was involuntarily following the movement of the herd
   funneled along the concrete pillars past the

Animatronic wax figure Obama in the window
    then kettled in a mall. This megalith lodged
the city's gods and dead the guidebook said but
    all I saw were *schickie-mickies* window-shopping
at the familiar retail outlets until one façade stood out:
    a heart-shaped face with pouty lips enclosed in a
tangle of red hair eyes framed by chunky black glasses
    any poet with an eye for detail could identify as

Céline. Ana slouched on the counter and tapped
        on her phone to a trust-fund manager lunching in
Köln. One by one her credit cards had been declined.
        She raised her chin and stared back as I added
some lines to a poem: *this is the last city / they will
        ever dream / soon security forces will / line
them up in rows / on city streets / looking for papers and
        weapons / I will bury my gun / in the park / in the*

Dream / try to flee but I will / be caught with the other
     debtors / who followed the flows of / easy money
and low rent / to the outer islands / or as far / as they could /
     get from the cultivation / of a political life.
With this my work was done so I exited the scene through
     the loading bay doors at the back of the food
court caught the first tram I saw let it transport me
     to this terminal in the Copytime in X-berg.

5

Dream Reels

City of speculation under a digital sky
    borderless slum of addiction and betrayal
a dream of Dreadful Night — I was in search
    of an exit. The taxis and buses would not stop
misshapen bodies wandered in every direction
    drugged and confrontational. I tried to use my phone
but it was frozen on a game I did not understand.
    My friends and lovers had abandoned me

At 3:00 am the century was still washed
    in an oily industrial twilight. Postcard quality
panopticism yet all techniques had failed to control
    the pageant these mutoid figures made. Nothing
rationalized surveyed designed approved
    derelict tenements spilling fresh corpses into streets
belonging to the black market. A single cop
    wandering stupid and disheveled with a target

On his head. This must have been day residue —
　　the last instance of an unfolding reciprocal relationship
between several sites mediated by the news. I was
　　in Baltimore Athens Berlin Syracuse London
Oakland Cairo Vancouver keeping my *Dream Notes*
　　on repressed collective desire. In retrospect I see
all the usual phantasms were there — Benjamin's
　　curtains filling and falling in the wind

Khatib's overcoat on the back of the door
　　　Weil's copy of *The Iliad* on the desk beside a
cup belonging to Villon. Heaps of furniture tossed
　　　from the balconies smoldered in the alley below.
On the corner a woman stood with a single coin
　　　in her outstretched hand as the river surged
before her. Members of a local triad directed
　　　the scene from a parked car. From this refuse I

Derived my heroic subjects not from the multitude
        as such. I believed it was my task to metabolize
not to document or arbitrate the terrain. The ghetto
        river rushed violently beneath the financial district
carving shaping burrowing past a shopping centre
        fringed with highrises down into a vast reservoir
of shit. The air was sour and stagnant. Children
        and persons without papers fished from the edges

Of the cisterns dredging up evidence of the familiar
    dispositifs as well as cigarette butts pens obsolete
navigational devices computers cellular phones all
    the goods and services that keep us in our sectors.
The promise of beauty was being destroyed block
    by block every flimsy tower every intimacy
every map every clock bending to the surge of
    the twentieth century then snapping at the base.

In another dream I found myself on a bus shooting
        footage of a pre-conceptualist Vancouver for a
documentary film an encyclopedia of clichéd
        cinematic objects reeling by in anticipation
of the speed to come — trees mountains trees
        mountains totem pole totem pole First Narrows
the fountain in the park pedestrians crossing and
        crossing again at an intersection in the centre

Of the city. It was lunch hour in 1973. Buskers
    busked on every corner. Chinatown was still populated.
Cowboys and Indians informed the fashions and
    behaviours of the new counter-culture while
bunker oil oozed onto the shores. This was the
    landscape of my reveries. A strange desire
urged my mind to banish as irregular all organic
    life and I was pleased with what my lens had done.

I watched this film and saw the intoxicating
        monotony of glass water steel cement
endless staircases and parking lots joining
        to form a long labyrinth which led to a
plaza. The fountains there were gushing silicon
        and sweat. Their heavy cataracts like curtains
did not fall as liquid should but hung frozen
        reified in the conditioned air while neutered

Figures with elongated breasts gazed at
    the clarity of their reflections in the display
cases. Groves of security cameras not trees
    fringed the deep pool where nothing stirred
except the flickering coins amassing at its base.
    I felt compelled to redirect the waters that fed this
scene so I made the water course under another
    culvert and every color every surface became

Prismatic. But when I woke my mind bright with
    flame I saw immediately the cheap and shabby
room I rented and the facts of my dislocated being
    came flowing back into my mind — the sirens
the screams on the streets under a sulphuric sky
    the rain bearing down upon a lethargic
colonial city. Note: to dream this way is to
    admit at last that we cannot accept our fate.

6
An Opening

I remember you from the riots: we
        were lost in the same wandering crowd
greeted each other not as anonymous
        allies — you said we were on the contrary
each other's premise and confirmation
        and should no longer act like strangers
because we had rid ourselves of *those birds* —
        but accomplices. And I remember a pact:

We said we were neither mass nor multitude
    nor making any demands to *reinvent the city*
but singular lives charting lines of flight from
    all their checkpoints campaigns milieus.
Thronging down Georgia our attention was absorbed
    by new objects new movements new events
and in the glaring eyes of the Griffons I
    remember you said the scene resembled

A *murder of crows dropping down from the sky*
    a passage from some poem I had written
years ago. We'd hooked up with that festive mob
    because we felt an affinity with its organs
of force. The citizens lined up on the other side of
    the street snapped pictures and gawked
as we consolidated our intimacies slipped off
    each other's belts and shoes and set them

In the grey plastic bins before passing through
        yet another full body scanner. That's how
an assemblage penetrates flesh — how Woolf's
        leaden circles could have dissolved in the air
— how mapping a city with paramours could be
        portrayed as an act of collective defense
not flâneurism — how the transition from window
        shopping to window smashing is theorized

In Constant's "Tract on Fenestration" — *the creation*
    of new openings in the urban labyrinth
to take the place of the old passages
    long since occluded by commerce and work
requires a move from the consumption of goods
    and services to their immediate
apprehension and redistribution — written in June
    1968. By Valentine's Day 2010 our passages

Were not about space but territory not politics
    but police borders bodies while debates
about *acts* were completely saturated in the icy
    Vancouver rain that fell for days and weeks
through the aftershocks. I remember the plum trees
    blossomed early that year. Certain residents
argued that their city was not ready for the violent
    aesthetic bloom of soft to dark pink

Said such spontaneous eruptions were unseasonal
        should never have materialized before
the conditions were correct: Winter then Spring
        he said. Red then amber. Amber then green
followed by red again. These codes channel the flow
        of cargo traffic desire to its appropriate
outlets and ports. One who enters this City
        from the South must travel North along Clark

Past Venables to Stewart then East into the Harbour
    just as the streams channeling beneath
the grid flow from the cemetery down Fraser
    and Main until they empty into False Creek.
At night the water here is still and dark reflects the
    towers of glass with their halogen bulbs until
the rain falls and the current swells to unsettle
    the image as though it were the city's dream.

7

Hospice

Woke up to sirens and left my room to walk the
    Eastside's dead streets of fog and carbon rime
joined a few other patients on a route devised
    to maximize invisibility. There is a lesson here
about politics I noted in the *Dream Notes*
    in an annotation made beside a faded photograph
of a building in X-Berg. Now it appears again
    projected on the Doggy Day Care across from

The Living Room on Powell. I noticed the shit on
      the sidewalk became less frequent travelling west
until it just vanished around Cambie not far from
      where the squat had been declared a public health
emergency in 2004. This civic septic system may be
      Vancouver but the structure of feeling is the same as
San Francisco's. Across the territories the settler atmosphere
      remains stagnant. We enter one operatory or another

Gnossienne No. 1 mixed with a lo-fi trap beat
	plays on a loop to grease the procedure. I can hear it
behind every little thing every hiss of steam every
	laugh every command posed as a question.
In the café they fixed their coffees to go talking of
	Murakami's *Ego*. Each utterance the cadence
of their speech the pauses silences duration of vowels
	repeated lexical units disclosed an affinity

Between language and urban planning. This became clearer
        as we approached the park — my words felt housed
in pre-fabricated concepts like the windows on the towers
        along Georgia reflecting a bloodshot October dawn.
To say the city is composed of such windows is to believe
        the city is a window: an opening made in a form
to oblige a sky stretched across a plane of intersecting lines
        that are streets carrying bodies to benches by a fountain

In a park where the premium medium-green trees and shrubs
    mix-and-matched in multiple varieties and textures
arranged in clusters with intermixed autumnal foliage
    gave the scene a superior realism in the brochures.
The plastic ducks on the board the joggers and cyclists
    were all to scale. I knew this theme park well. Like
the other nomads fleeing the OPD programs of the
    mid-90s I found myself here often forced

To learn the new habitus new rituals new codes of
        the Statistical Life to survive in a post-human city
of quarantines. The trick was to walk along the fences
        that separated the camps while remaining lucid
about what side one was on. Some of us were caught
        trying to escape and were put to work repairing
the gates some were caught at the entry points and expelled
        to secondary enclosures where they salvaged

Obsolete literary and political distractions while others
     accepted even aestheticized the new forces said
precarity was a superior mode of life — all flow.
     In the East Bay we had concluded that every program
every platform every deal propping up the infrastructure
     was to be burned. Actually the districts and zones are
precincts built for the cops until they are recomposed
     as *terrain* — the squares the malls even the hospitals

Where the white tiled hallways are glazed with surplus
        biological juices will belong to us. Through one window
you might perceive a client cleaning her stumps. Through
        another a flash of purple cock. The exits from the
organ transplant units are soiled with *hostis*. You won't see it
        so much as feel it in your lower back. The sensation
will rise up and explode from your mouth in a plume
        of streets wires arteries and trams.

8

Requiem
(for Hammertown)

Drifting on Church St. I saw astonishing buildings
     being demolished by the forces of will and fate.
Corvus perched on a chain link fence head tilted eyes
     salient as the fortifications crumbled. In this city
heritage buildings — new swag of the creative class —
     crumble and fall while ravens watch. Prime plus
on the mortgage and ceilings collapse. Towers fall
     and will fall again. Structures faded by exchange

Break away sink into the shafts to join the union
     of unremembered dead who turn to coal beneath
our feet. Tent cities also come and go. Torched
     and tagged these walls outlasted the strikes
remained unmoved by social force. The value housed
     in architecture proved more resilient than labour
I noted in the *Journal*. Photographic evidence shows
     the financiers in their quarters holding

Parties and banquets in halls with servants while
    their enemies were hanged from a crag across the bay.
Since 1852 the sound of the police set the tempo
    in this town until fate cut in. The dead rest on both sides
of Albert St. now. I swerve south on Milton
    follow an aberrant line to Medea and Hecate
off the city grid down into the Cat Stream Ravine.
    In this chthonic zone I unearthed my materials —

In the foreground black diamond dust coats
    the park bench by the railroad crossing signal
side streets static in the fog. The background recedes
    the lines wires telephone poles rails carry
the eye away from the intersection and head up island.
    Split level homes in pink stucco behind the magnolia
the brittle stems of the fennel gone to seed are tangled
    with blackberries among the alders. Across the ravine

New suburban homes press against each other
  under a flattened sky. Broken bottles shotgun shells
coffee cups a fragment of brick. So much refuse here.
  Soiled blue sleeping bag discarded in the riverbed
water pooling on a corner lot cleared for some future
  development beside the former miners' homes
shingle siding with windows covered in PVC
  branches and scavenged wood heaped in the yard.

The neighbors have moved away. A fallow community
    garden built among disassembled interlocking concrete
blocks. Children live here too. They use salvaged materials
    to build structures in the trees play their games among
the sodden tarps and mattresses bright green moss
    growing on the asphalt. Not even the billboards are leased.
The blossoms on the cherry tree suggest change but it's not
    possible to tell where industry ends and the city begins.

The photographs prove that every neighborhood is middle
    class. Painted cedar slab fences separate their homes
only the streams and the alleyways are civic. He rents
    a room in the Diplomat Motel drinks at the Mount Benson
Legion takes the bus to the pool then climbs for a view
    looking down on the *new suburban homes*. Once again
the discarded tires orange security fencing cement
    blocks fennel blackberries alders and rocks. At the cross-

Walk the light turns green a cyclist passes. Through the
    window on the bus he sees the empty soccer fields the
space for lease above the cash store the Vietnamese place
    on Bowen Rd. sees the willow trees behind The Willows
housing complex. The women waiting for the bus did not speak
    to him or to each other but it's not the same image over and
over again with different depth angles filters — only the fog
    and the hand that held the camera remain the same.

9

Exodus
(Via Dione)

One of the transverse routes I took
　　while fleeing another of these metropolitan
mazes spilled into a scene of semi-rusticated
　　columns and second-order Ionic pilasters
framing a square. Hard lines here. A few feet
　　further the statue exploded from the cobble-
stones: Arethusa's escape presided over
　　by Artemis — *Diana is hard / but her breasts*

Sometimes are cloudy — with peaks of black
    driving the tip of her head towards the sky
the warm wind the rain. A staircase in the
    open air led to a gallery behind large
iron gates and ladders to cages perched on top
    of slender columns. The clocks had stopped
at exactly 5:00 in the afternoon 30 April
    2019. The sky worked through varying hues

Of copper to silver as I returned to Room 514
    to rearrange my experiences. No phone
no hotspot no books just a bed and a chair
    in a studio with a desk supporting a model
of a miniature city: trams towers pedestrians
    all behaving as intended. I had fabricated
everything here — signs streets letters
    in stone — knowing we are coterminous

With where we stand. Along the borders of my city
    I had placed identical horizontal blocks
made visible a zone of tension reclaimed the savage
    exterior as a form exemplary of my sovereign power.
I reached to pull the blinds down against the ceaseless
    rain. No light except from the campfires on rooftops
candles illuminating the tenement windows across
    Dunlevy. I refuse to praise the abstract laws

Of the city — the separations the techniques of control
the towers with their stone steps the flow of
money cascading up staircases reaching towards
sterile lofts that redefine vertical marginality
as class mobility — so I shall locate my small scenes
of insurrection not on the horizontal outskirts
of the city but in its central core. These sublime
if solitary masquerades where bottles full

Of gasoline mixed with Vaseline set in rows
     near upturned newspaper boxes dragged into
streets to block the passage the flow the circulation
     of goods and services as the Owl of Minerva
spreads its wings on an unresisting urban wind
     are part poetic ingenuity part inevitable laws
of history congealing in two parts hallucination
     and one part fragmentary individual

Experience. In other words my materials are

    real but their affects are imitations. The radiator
in the corner of the room bangs and whistles

    as the water rises through the pipes and the form
expands. In the predawn dark I noted this in

    a section of the *Journal* dedicated to comparing
selected passages from Spinoza and Debord on the

    confluence of what is fabricated and what is felt

And when I asked what is the meaning of this city
    you replied — "we are not entirely flesh
we are an unsettled throng composed of unstable
    elements clad in alloys concrete glass
surging through a grid until an opening forms
    in the labyrinth of bone in which we lodge.
From here we began our course so here we will
    return one crowded Monday morning in May."

Acknowledgements

I acknowledge the Snuneymuxw territory I write from, and am grateful to be living on.

I am fortunate to have a few am-coms put their eyes to this book: Dianna Bonder, fellow traveller and co-conspirator; Danielle LaFrance, who keeps "it" real; Reg Johanson and Aaron Vidaver, who I always write for. Many others in the cramped poetic space of Vancouver, the islands of the Salish Sea, and south on the I5, are interlocutors here, often unwittingly.

Thanks to Michael Barnholden and Mercedes Eng for their eyes and ears.

Thanks to Finn for his work on the video poem for the book.

I acknowledge Peter Culley, whose photographs of Nanaimo included in the Black Diamond Dust exhibition are the "materials" in Canto VIII.

Thanks to Rolf Maurer and New Star.

Finally I acknowledge the support of the Canada Council for the Arts and Access Copyright for providing grants that assisted with the composition of this book.

For Rebecca Davey (1944 – 2017).

Vimeo: vimeo.com/citystill